THE YOUTUBE ALGORITHM

THE YOUTUBE ALGORITHM

Decoding the Mystery

ROWAN EVERHART

QuantumQuill Press

CONTENTS

CHAPTER 1

Introduction

Featuring the most popular video-hosting website, the research aims to decipher the code that lies within this algorithm. Perhaps the social media users who leverage popularity from YouTube would be of primary interest, however the main reason for conducting this research is to allow public access to information. There are many different ways to abuse the importance of YouTube to broadcast advertising, fake videos, malware, etc. This paper would allow the public to be more informed about what is truly popular and why it's difficult to avoid popularity schemes based on the various factors that are configured into the popularity of a video. Often times these schemes use botnets to simulate views/clicks on videos to increase their popularity. Completing an analysis of the YouTube would give us a better understanding of these schemes and allow for protection against artificially inflated popular videos. This topic is chosen with a curious mind, to discover if we can truly distinguish the difference between organic popularity and artificially stimulated popularity. As many social media users know, the fame of PSY's Gangnam Style had earned him $2,000,000 from a whopping 3,862,515,905 views as of June 2014. This might come off as a great success when it reality was just a smart business move by a video recruiting a farm of botnets to increase the view count. At the time, YouTube's most popular video is Justin Beiber's "Baby" with 1,173,639,173 views, however this number may be disputed when comparing organic popularity to artificial. With PSY's success and cash reward, YouTube could have arguably refunded his video with rebates intended for sharing in ad revenue from such a popular video. Should this be considered success? This research would allow YouTube and social media users to analyze if these videos are truly popular and why.

CHAPTER 2

Understanding YouTube's Algorithm

The exact functionality of YouTube's algorithm is kept secret and changes periodically. At its core, the system works to predict the likelihood that a viewer will click on a video and watch it for a long period of time. The video sharing site is able to suggest more videos to viewers and make videos more visible by placing them on the homepage when a user is more likely to click on suggested videos rather than searching for a particular video or visiting a certain channel. An increase in a video's click-through rate (CTR) in combination with an increase in a user's session time on YouTube due to an increase in suggested video CTR leads to a net increase in total views for the video and a net increase in ad revenue for the content producer.

In order to maximize viewership and ad revenue, it is necessary that content producers understand how the system works and what factors are most important in predicting visibility on viewers' homepages and recommended video lists. A good understanding of the system can also put into perspective the types of videos most likely to be affected by any updates and what part of the user base is most likely to view an individual's content.

Importance of the Algorithm

A key part of understanding YouTube's algorithm is understanding why it matters. The algorithm's role is to rank what videos are suggested to users. If your video is ranked higher, its chance of being clicked on and viewed increases dramatically. For example, if video A is searched by a user, and video A is ranked higher than video B, then video A is more likely to be clicked on, even if videos A and B are about the same topic. Also, if video B is related to video A, then video B will likely be suggested to the user at a later time. If the user has a clear interest in the topic of video A, then they are likely to watch and enjoy video B. This is valuable for the content creator of video B, as their video will gain a new viewer who is genuinely interested in the content. If video B had a low ranking and did not appear in the suggestions, it is possible the user may never find or watch video B, even though they may have enjoyed it. This entire process also has a cumulative effect, as for video B to reach a high rank it will likely have been clicked on and viewed from various other sources multiple times. Since user retention is the key element of the algorithm, the more the user enjoys video B, the higher the rank video B will achieve.

Factors Influencing the Algorithm

Engagement is another important factor, and in this scenario, engagement refers to the video's retention rate. This is the amount of time a viewer spends watching a video, usually expressed as a percentage. If a video has a strong retention rate compared to other videos on similar topics, it is likely to be recommended. An exact number was not disclosed, but it was said that high retention videos are likely to be recommended to a viewer looking at similar videos.

Video content quality is the most important factor. YouTube serves video recommendations to viewers based on the quality and content of the video they are watching. This means that if a video has a higher retention rate compared to other videos of a similar topic, it will be recommended more frequently, which brings us to the next factor.

Algorithm Updates and Changes

One problem with such frequent and obscure changes to the algorithm is the predictability of their impact. YouTube Partners, a forum for users who are eligible to apply for revenue sharing, often complain of dramatic changes to viewership and channel growth with no explanation. Such events can be particularly disheartening for a content creator who has to re-strategize on their SEO and marketing. When changes to the algorithm result in a negative impact for a particular website or user group, it is not uncommon for public outcry and Google bomb tactics to reverse the decision; a situation which has occurred a number of times throughout Google's past.

YouTube states, "We are always experimenting and launching new features and products to help you see more videos you care about and make fewer videos you don't." Although it is impossible to know exactly how many changes they make annually, it is clear that alterations to the algorithm are frequent and ongoing. This isn't surprising for a number of reasons, but primarily as technology and user trends are constantly changing. What may have worked well for a period of time may become redundant and in need of replacement. For example, in the early days of YouTube, tag stuffing was a common black hat tactic in which a video was loaded with numerous tags to increase searchability. This was largely stopped when Google put emphasis on clearer, high-quality metadata for videos.

CHAPTER 3

The Role of Engagement

Watch time and session duration are two of the best indirect measures of engagement. They are a proxy for the real value a user attaches to the video. They are a measure of satisfaction because the viewer wouldn't continue watching a video that they don't enjoy. If a video is compelling, users may spend some time going to the creator's channel to look at more content. This behavior is captured by session duration, or the length of time a user spends on the site after viewing a video. High watch time and session duration can lead to improved search, Suggested, and Recommended results for a video. So, creators can improve video performance by encouraging viewers to watch more videos.

Engagement is the degree of a user's psychological investment in a given entity. It is a good proxy for the user's positive or negative experience. All of the user's online touches with the entity can be considered elements of engagement. The key to improving engagement is improving the user's experience. Likes, comments, and shares are the most direct ways that a viewer can engage with a video. While YouTube has had some form of like/dislike feature since 2005, the ability to leave comments was added in late 2006, and the ability to share a video with external social media platforms was added in late 2008.

Likes, Comments, and Shares

For this work on engagement, I used my alternative accounts and one of them is subscribed to my main channel. This was done to prevent bias caused by suggested videos, as the related videos algorithm may suggest different videos based on a variable such as likes, and thus skew the view data.

One video was a vlog, another was a gaming video, and the other was a highly professional video about global warming. Using different types of videos allowed me to analyze the effect of engagement on different styles of video. Content was tested by manipulating variables, with the goal of determining the effect of likes, comments, and shares on a video.

Creators have been curious about whether or not likes, comments, and shares affect a video's success on YouTube. In order to show what role engagement plays in the YouTube algorithm, I compared 3 videos.

3.1. Likes, Comments, and Shares

Watch Time and Session Duration

Measuring a video's watch time against videos of a similar length, to avoid giving preference to longer videos, is expressed as a percentage. In this way, the expected quality of longer videos can be compared fairly to shorter videos. High watch time retention on a video usually shows that the video is of retention and high audience satisfaction. While the viewer may not have enjoyed a longer video enough to watch the entire thing, the video being good quality would be expressed by the watch time percentage before the viewer stopped watching.

The simplest way to understand the importance of "watch time" in algorithms is to compare it to the rating. The more your audience likes it, the more likely it is to be recommended. And if a viewer enjoys one video, the likelihood of them enjoying a similar video is quite high. Therefore, the watch time is important on the video being viewed, as well as future recommendations.

Click-Through Rate (CTR) and Video Thumbnails

Secondly, Thumbs up/Down! The act of rating has an easier definition. The more thumbs up a video has in comparison to the down, the better the video rates. Although it might not seem too relevant to the act of clicking on a video and will be covered in terms of video progression at a later stage, it is worth mentioning here that like the CTR, it will likely provoke more viewing from the user and more favorable videos in the future. In addition to providing direct feedback to video creators, likes and dislikes ultimately influence the relationship between video and user by shaping suggested content and search rankings.

Having observed the role of viewing patterns and subscriptions in the prior sections, the next step to understanding the YouTube algorithm is comprehension of what it takes for a user to click on a video, be it from their homepage, the search page, or a shared link. The first necessary concept is Click-Through Rate (CTR). This is measured by the probability of a user clicking on a video. Using a large sample size of impressions, CTR = (clicks/impressions) is easily calculable on individual videos or channels. Considering a high CTR means it's more likely a user will continue onto other content by the same creator or view related content. This is an entirely positive outcome, but the formula for CTR, depicting clicks directly over impressions, means it may be hard to distinguish a good rate from clickbait.

CHAPTER 4

Content Quality and Relevance

It's a safe bet that much of this is studied through human inter-action, not by a computer. Since the algorithm seeks to mimic the behavior of a typical user, it makes sense that it should work to get the most entertaining video to the top. On this basis, the most we can glean is that the algorithm mirrors another study into user be-havior in order to best determine what sets videos apart. This study came up with the concept of "seeking" and "broadcasting," which is quite relevant to YouTube. A "broadcasting" video is one that's more likely to be linked to others and viewed as an essential part of the site, whereas a "seeking" video may be an obscure piece or something like amateur music videos; something that definitely has a market but isn't necessarily strongly connected to the rest of the site. Step 1.2 is to content quality as it's aimed at the desired action of the user.

Research and common sense both dictate that quality content is more likely to gain better viewership. This seems to hold true with the algorithm. On a fundamental level, content quality can't cur-rently be measured by an algorithm. YouTube has understandably been quite secretive about exactly how they rank quality, not so much from an SEO perspective but in the difference between a video with millions of views and one with millions of views and thousands of subscribers, an engaged community, and a high level of retention.

Video Title and Description

The video title is obviously an important determiner of how well the video is likely to perform. Apart from brand presence, the wording of a title will determine the ease of its findability by the search engine. If the video is the latest in a popular series, then including the series name is vital, even neglecting to do so on one video can result in a significant drop in views on that video. This is because the viewer enjoyed the last video of the series and searched for the next one, and could not find it. The video title should be kept to the point and not be too long, as shorter titles are easier to read and retain in the memory. A clear and clever title may win a click through from a browse pages and a good title will increase the chance of a viewer watching another video straight after the first. If the video belongs to a genre, let's play for example, including the genre in the video can be important when trying to attract viewer looking for that type of content. The video title's importance in relation to SEO is how most search engines give the greatest weight to the first word of the title. So if the video is related to a popular or a trending topic, it may be more beneficial to include that as the first word of the title, rather than the name of the video. This does mean that we have to carefully consider whether we make any kind of sacrifice to the integrity of our brand, if it's at the cost of the clarity or representations of the video content.

Tags and Keywords

While tags are usually the go-to form of metadata for search algorithms, a potentially underused tactic can be to use closed captions. This also has the effect of increasing accessibility, especially to those who are hard of hearing or deaf. According to Google, syncing the transcripts with the video provides the algorithm with more information to index, and can give the videos a higher relevance for the keywords used within the transcript. Although this is also very time-consuming, it can be quite effective in more competitive search targets. This can be seen as a parallel to the use of metadata in webpages and indexing.

While tags and keywords are not an overly important factor in the algorithm, they are pivotal in the process of the video being indexed by search engine spiders. This has the potential to increase the accessibility of the video as well as increasing the volume of viewers. So how can one maximize this process? According to YouTube, the best way to add tags and keywords is to use phrases that are highly relevant to the video content but also very popular search targets. A good way to increase the prominence of your tags will be to use them as video responses to videos which are highly related and have high viewership. It is also said that adding singular tags at the bottom of the tag list may increase the prominence of all the tags in the list. An example of this would be adding a tag "fighter" and "plane" "pilot" in separate tag lists then using "fighter plane pilot" in separate tags.

Video Transcripts and Closed Captions

Closed captions are also considered to be text data in the eyes of a search engine. According to a help page for uploading closed captions, files YouTube will use this info for ranking your videos for searching in any relevant queries. Since not all content on YouTube is captioned, this gives a huge advantage to the videos that do have captions.

Search engines can read and index the text of a transcript. It can't watch a video, listen to the audio, or determine what it is about with any great accuracy. That gives content owners a way to tell the search engines exactly what is said in their videos. If done well, it can improve the chances of the video ranking highly in search results and being found by more viewers.

Audio content is not currently searchable by a search engine. The closest thing the search engine has is found on the upload page under Video Analysis. It says, "This feature automatically extracts information about the contents of your video. In the future, it will be used to drive new discovery and monetization features." Although that may bring much value in the future, it is not currently available to the public. Using transcripts has been a popular video search engine optimization technique for a couple of years now.

CHAPTER 5

Viewer Retention and Interaction

Cards are small notifications that appear on the top right of a video. They can be used to promote any content on the channel from playlists to polls. If a viewer clicks a card, it counts as a card click rate. Cards are effective to persuade a viewer to watch another video while they are still watching the current video. A video with a higher card click rate has a better chance of getting recommended with other videos by the same creator.

End screens and cards are an important way to keep a viewer on your channel. End screens are a feature added in 2016 that allows the creator to promote up to four elements (videos, channels, or playlists) to be displayed for the final 5-20 seconds of a video. These elements can be shown on a mobile device, computer, and TV, allowing viewers to easily click on the content. If a viewer clicks on an end screen element, it counts as an element click rate. If the viewer is directed to another video by the same creator through an end screen, the next video will have a better chance of being recommended to the viewer.

Audience retention is the amount of a video someone watches. If someone only watches the first 15 seconds of a five-minute video, the audience retention is very low. A viewer coming from an external website has the same value as a viewer coming from within YouTube. The best way to increase audience retention is to produce high-quality videos that viewers will want to watch from beginning to end. If a video has high audience retention, YouTube promotes the video through search and recommended videos, and the creator has a greater chance of more views.

Audience Retention

In all cases, it is imperative to keep the user watching videos.

In another light, a user who has experienced a satisfying viewing session on YouTube is of higher expected value to Google. This user is more likely to return in the future and spend more time on the site. This person is also closer to becoming a loyal user. Loyal users are considered separately in the recommendation system as there is evidence that they are more likely to rate videos.

This situation is expected to happen less for an experienced user with the new 2D grid delivery system. However, the 2D grid does not affect the fact that the uploader wants to keep the user on his video and showing less content to a user is less likely to increase the amount they watch.

A recommendation system aims to select the best videos to show a user. If a user is likely to abandon a video for another, the best action for the recommendation system is to not initially suggest the video they were going to abandon. This would be disastrous from the video uploader's point of view. He has already enticed the user to view the video, showing the video to the user was a success. The uploader does not want to lose this user at the end of the video. He wants the user to watch the video and then another of his to further increase the probability of the user continuing to the future.

Leaving aside the button, everything on the watch page is designed around viewer retention. As mentioned earlier, YouTube optimizes everything to increase net watch time. When this is compared to effort in developing recommendation systems, it is clear how crucial watch time is.

End Screens and Cards

Unfortunately, for smaller channels who are most likely to experience trouble with viewer retention, End Screens are not unlocked as a feature until the channel is monetized. This can be quite discouraging, but I can understand the logic behind it. YouTube does not want the server processing power that goes into analyzing and suggesting videos to essentially be wasted on content that is not generating ad revenue.

YouTube offers two methods of attempting to direct viewers to another of the channel's videos: End Screens and Cards. End Screens are a handy tool that YouTube added, allowing you to suggest another of the channel's videos during the last 5-20 seconds of your video. This can be used to keep viewers on your content binge or to direct them to specific content you believe they would be interested in after analyzing their behavior (in my case, I was analyzing how to use End Screens on my video about End Screens to see if it would cause more people to watch the whole thing).

Community Interaction and Subscriber Growth

By keeping viewers absorbed in content creators' videos and having them as eager to know as much as possible about the channel and updates, they are more likely to subscribe. Subscriptions, of course, in the form of an engaged viewer, are the result of wanting to keep up to date with a content provider's latest videos. Therefore, anything that can increase the drive to subscribe or the visibility of a channel's subscription button is an indirect method to further increase viewer retention.

Uploading content and leaving the site will cause diminishing returns in growing a viewer base. This is known as the 'dead period' where no interaction can occur. Therefore, the more a user does to keep traffic of their return viewers high, the more YouTube will promote their channel. New features such as posting bulletins and mobile text notifications for upload updates help facilitate this.

Interaction between content creators and viewers is vital for the growth of a channel community and subscriber base. In line with the rest of YouTube's features, videos that enable community interaction and return visits from viewers are favored. Regular releases encourage viewers to come back to watch the latest videos. A channel is seen as more of an active community than a soapbox for one person, therefore viewers get more attached to the content as well as the person delivering said content.

CHAPTER 6

The Power of Recommendations

Recommendations come in five basic forms. The first and most familiar to casual viewers is the related video section. These videos are cherry picked by YouTube's algorithm, gathered by comparing factors such as the video's content, tags, and video name to other videos. The next is the in-video overlay ad. Those are self-explanatory. (As an interesting note, until 2008 advertisements were chosen based on the user's previous search history). Third is the homepage video suggestion. Videos are targeted from a user's entire history; however, the result is more effective on frequent users. Subscriptions are sometimes overshadowed by more recent content by subscription box warriors, making the homepage a defacto subscription page for better or worse. The fourth type are notifications on mobile and the YouTube app. This has a significant impact due to the high percentage of mobile users. The last type are emails, the rarest recommendation seen.

The YouTube recommendation engine is what makes the site so addicting. It's a video equivalent of the StumbleUpon button.

As of writing, it's made its way to the front page as well. The "What to Watch" section is a litmus test of a given viewer's tastes, determined by past viewed content. As more data is collected on a user, this section will generate more accurate results. This ultimately leads to increased time on the site. A staggering 70% of watch time is attributed to the recommendation engine; that's a lot of power. With such a large margin, an improvement in recommendations will have a profound effect on what content goes viral and what becomes a dead channel.

Related Videos and Suggested Content

These playlists of suggested content can often keep the user on the site longer than if they were to continuously search for new videos after each one they finish watching. This is due to the high relevance of suggested content to what the user is interested in at the time. The amount of time a successful algorithm can keep a user on a site is a known measure of user engagement; therefore, this feature of keeping users on the site is very powerful.

The related videos on the video watch page can often lure a user into a long binge of videos as they keep clicking the next suggested video. Similarly, the videos that appear on the user's page can some-times be so relevant to what the user is interested in at the time that the user keeps watching videos from this playlist for an extended period of time. This occurs commonly with video game content and tutorial videos.

A large component of the YouTube platform that has received relatively little attention is its related video and suggested video features. These two aspects of the site involve videos that appear on the right-hand column of the page when a user clicks on a video, and the videos that appear in a playlist on the user's page when they are watching a video from their subscriptions. It is often the case that these videos are more prominently featured to the user than the videos on their personal feed.

Personalized Recommendations

This is a rather difficult task mainly because "the right time" is a fairly intangible concept and is likely to differ from one user to the next. An extreme case would be a user wanting to watch some light-hearted content when they are, in fact, feeling frustrated or upset. So there is potential that the user will not click a video which is, in fact, the most satisfying at that time. Despite the intricacies, the fact that there is usually a "best video" out of those available to watch means the feed algorithm can assume an allocation problem. The decision variable is a binary variable for each video, specifying whether or not the video is included in the feed. Simulation of user watch probabilities can generate an objective function to maximize satisfaction, and due to the very large amount of videos on the website, only a minute fraction of possible feeds will be evaluated.

So how is this achieved? Well, to begin, each video on the user's feed is there because there was a certain probability that the user would watch it if it was recommended. The list was then generated by an algorithm with the goal of maximizing cumulative user satisfaction. In other words, the algorithm aims to show the right video to the user at the right time, such that the user is most likely to watch it, and it is, in doing so, satisfying for the user.

In 2013, YouTube introduced a page for users to view and edit their own personalized feed of videos from the homepage, as well as their mobile devices. This feed is a simple list of videos yet can be very powerful in terms of utilizing the recommendation system. The general concept of a personalized feed is to show the user a list of videos, ideally tailored to the user's unique and changing interests, in an order that is most satisfying for the user to watch. This is different from a search list or an auto-play queue in that the videos are aimed to be chosen without the user having to make further decisions, and the satisfaction optimization is aimed to increase the chance the user will watch the next video recommended.

YouTube's Explore and Trending Pages

Though both pages aim to assist users in finding new content, they are essentially marketing tools for popular videos/channels and are not a true attempt to help users find 'new' content. The Explore page provides users with recommendations of videos that are popular across the platform and trending at that time. The Trending page goes a step further to recommend videos that are very popular in the user's own country. When comparing the two pages, they are essentially the same concept with the Trending page targeting a more specific demographic.

The Explore page is found at the bottom of YouTube's mobile apps and helps users of the platform to broaden their online experience. According to YouTube, the page allows users to "Discover new videos and topics on your Home screen." The Trending page is hosted on YouTube's main site and is designed to help individuals find the most popular videos.

CHAPTER 7

Strategies for Algorithm Success

Optimizing metadata is essentially optimizing your video information to make it easier to find and more appealing to the YouTube algorithm. As a general rule, you want your video information to be both accurate and meaningful while being concise. If your information is accurate then people will be able to find what they are looking for and if it's meaningful and concise then there'll be incentive to click and watch the video. The most important aspect of metadata is your title. Always make sure that you are using a descriptive and accurate title. Be honest about your video and never use a title that is misleading because it may deter viewers from watching your other content. Titles also allow for use of keywords. Keywords are useful words that define the topic and genre of your content. An example of a keyword would be something like "tutorial". Titles and keywords not only make your content easier to find using the search bar, but YouTube may recommend it alongside other content of a similar nature. A good title and effective use of keywords can significantly increase traffic to your video. The title and keywords will also become strong determining factors for the relevance of your video, which decides whether you video shows up a search and where it ranks in comparison to other videos of a similar nature.

The strategies for algorithm success on YouTube differ from person to person and from video to video. One of those strategies for success is ensuring that your viewers are engaged. This is just a smart move for anyone that is creating videos; it's good to have engaging content. What people fail to realize is that the level of engagement between one video and its viewer can be difference between showing up in a search and being buried deep in the results. A viewer that is engaged in a video is more likely to watch the whole thing, and also likely to watch more content after the video is over. A good way to keep viewers engaged is to ask them a question or have a call to action at the end of each video. You can use annotations, video or a combination of the two. The more activity that your content generates, the more likely it is that you engaged the viewer.

Creating Engaging Content

Finally, now that viewers are notified of when new content is available, it is a good idea to work on consistency of future content to further increase the expectancy of a viewer's return.

Subscribers are notified weekly of channels they have subscribed to if new videos are available, but there is no feature that lets them know the exact time a video is released. To work around this, release the video as unlisted and then change the video to public once it would have appeared in subscription boxes. This can easily be discovered by viewing the video's analytics.

An often overlooked method to engage the viewer is to let them know the benefits of subscribing to your channel at the start or end of a video. Viewers are more likely to subscribe if they feel they will benefit from doing so, so if the content you provide has already built value in their mind then it's a good time to let them know.

ADEPT (Attention, Interest, Desire, Action, Post-action) is a sales framework developed in 1921 which can be used to construct a guideline to achieving a conversion in any sales process. With regards to YouTube, it basically ends up as creating and maintaining viewer attention through successful immersion in content, until the desired action is to return for more content. A good understanding of ADEPT and application of its principles is an excellent way to maintain audience retention throughout a video or series of videos.

There are several ways to make your content more engaging, the first of which is to hook the viewer in the first 15 seconds. YouTube analytics now shows detailed statistics regarding audience retention, which can be used to identify at which points in a video viewers are most likely to navigate away. Videos with a good hook can expect to see a large drop off in retention right after the hook, though the goal is to keep the drop off as low as possible.

Engaging content is the key to success on YouTube as it determines how much of an individual video a viewer will watch and whether they will return for future videos. The more compelling the video, the higher the retention rate and the higher the likelihood of gaining a subscriber. The main focus of creating engaging content is to keep the viewer watching until the end. Videos with a large portion of their audience retention are more likely to appear in suggested videos.

Optimizing Metadata and Thumbnails

Thumbnails are the small, clickable snapshots that a viewer will see to get a preview of your video. An eye-catching custom thumbnail can dramatically affect your click-through rate on a suggested video, on the search results page, and as a related video. It is quite easy to take a high-quality snapshot from your video and use that as a thumbnail. However, if the snapshot is not particularly engaging or related to your video, it is a wasted opportunity. Instead, a graphic or picture replacing a video contains a more enticing graphical representation of what your video is about. However, it is against YouTube's terms of service to use a picture that is not a snapshot taken from your video, and it is rare but possible that YouTube will remove a video with a custom thumbnail that it deems inappropriate. A good custom thumbnail is striking and ideally a bit provocative. If it's something that just makes a user curious about what's going on in the video, then it has done its job.

In order for a video to surface as a suggested video and drive views through YouTube's algorithm, metadata and thumbnails must be optimized. Metadata is the information that conveys what your video is about, such as a video title, description, and tags. This information is critical for search and discovery. It helps users decide whether or not to watch your video, and it will affect how well your video ranks in search results. Titles should be compelling and an accurate reflection of your video content. Make sure your description is a solid 2-3 paragraphs and that you're utilizing all your given tags. The comments you place on your own and others' videos are vital as well. Uploading a video in response to another user's video will make the video a top response try to the original, and a recent video with a recent comment carries much more weight than an old video or comment. Finally, video tags are another way to help determine the relevance of your video. Try to use a mix of common and more specific tags, for example "soccer" and "UEFA cup 2011", but be wary inappropriate or excessive tags can result in the removal of your video or even your account from YouTube.

Building a Strong Community

An interesting tool provided by Google is the 'In-video programming' feature. It allows you to embed a promotion for another video across all of your content or at a specific instance. This can encourage cross-viewing of content and increase comments that are based around the work of both parties.

Community collaboration can also occur between creators with a similar fan base. Allocca made note of how patterns often form between similar groups of people that can lead to unexpected success in a specific location, age group, and even gender. This suggests that if creators with common viewers were to collaborate and share content, there will be a widespread effect that benefits both parties. This has been tested by a popular Gamers Let's Play channel using collaborations and shout outs. An analysis of the aggregate of his videos suggests that there is a large spike in views and comments corresponding with the date of collaboration.

Community collaboration generally takes advantage of the fact that videos which are shared tend to spread overwhelmingly. This would benefit a creator who has established a relationship with his audience as it encourages higher viewing figures and comments. Although in comparison to the other social media outlets discussed, Google+ is highly recommended due to the fact that linking a video to a relevant conversation can lead to a number of positive, detailed comments. This can help in deciphering the mystery as to why the algorithm promotes certain videos, as higher rankings can often appear. A case study of a Japanese cooking channel was presented to describe how establishing a strong community and having them link his videos to similar content lead to top video rankings.

As mentioned, the ability to have increased communication between creator and viewer is made far more accessible through Custom URLs. Additionally, the Channel Bulletins feature can be used to send updates to subscribers of your channel, notifying them of new videos or asking for their contributions and feedback. Creating a Facebook Fan Page was suggested by Google, claiming that sharing content and encouraging discussion to an active community can significantly alter the rate at which a video becomes viral.

In Kevin Allocca's TED Talk 'Why Videos Go Viral', the fact that social influence often causes growth to occur rapidly was highlighted. Community can be seen as the supportive fans and consumers behind your channel. They are likely to share your content, give positive feedback, and in this instance, significantly impact the algorithm's decision in promoting your videos. As higher watch time videos are more likely to appear on the home page, having a dedicated community that contributes to this will strongly benefit channel growth.

CHAPTER 8

Analyzing and Measuring Success

No one said becoming a global hit was easy. 'Evolution of Dance' success didn't happen overnight. It took Jason seven months to hit 50,000 views, but the momentum started to pick up and within the next few months he made his way to 50,000 views a day! Get a deeper understanding of who your audience is and how you can improve your content for them. Although Jason was initially creating content for a high school talent show, he found out who his real audience was and changed his content when he started to see his view and subscriber numbers increase. Jason also noticed the type of viewer he was attracting. He realized he had a global audience as people from all over the world were viewing and subscribing to his channel. This discovery led to a change in his image and what countries he would script his videos to. He could never have known this information without YouTube's analytic data. The majority of creating a successful brand or product is trial and error. If something doesn't work at first, change it until you find something that does work. Jason spent years experimenting and iterating the type of video he created and what his audience wanted. He had many failed attempts at doing series and thematic videos, but once he created the 'Evolution of Dance' it was an immediate hit and Jason knew he was on to something. Without the ability to measure performance, create low-cost scalable experiments, and make guided decisions, it's likely Jason would have never found his true audience and the success of the dance video. With the right level of effort, it will be possible for those trying to make a successful channel on YouTube, but it will not happen overnight. You have to be innovative, persistent, and can never be afraid of failure.

YouTube Analytics and Insights

YouTube Analytics is a statistics report that provides valuable information for creators to measure and analyze their performance. It offers a modern and quick way to understand who your audience is, what content is successful, and how they have grown over a selected time period. One of the most important features of YouTube Analytics is the ability to view interactive reports on how viewers found your content. The 'Traffic Sources' report provides data on how viewers are finding your site, with metrics on whether they came from YouTube search, clicked on suggested videos or playlists, or accessed your content through a YouTube partner site. Understanding how viewers are finding your content can provide creators with insight on whether strategies to promote their content, such as having other users recommend it through sharing on social networks or telling their friends by word of mouth, are actually working and leading to more views. By knowing what works, creators can amplify their successful promotion strategies and improve those that are not providing favorable results.

Tracking Metrics and Performance

Viral video expert suggests that before delving too deeply into data tracking and analysis, it's important to define what equates to success for your channel. You will be comparing your video's metrics against one another and also data from other similar channels, so having a good understanding of what you hope to achieve is essential to making sense of the data you gather. suggests asking yourself what your video is trying to get the viewer to think, feel, or do as a result of watching and what type of viewer behavior would be indicative of the video achieving this. This is useful for determining which metrics are most important to track.

One of the most basic and effective methods of tracking video performance is using a simple Excel spreadsheet to record specific metrics from the YouTube Insights page. The specific metrics that you may want to track are likely to vary between different channels, depending on what the specific goals of video content are. As a starting point, useful metrics include the number of views received and the rate of viewer retention across each video. This is useful for comparing the performance of different videos and identifying patterns or common characteristics among videos with high or low retention rates.

Analytics describes the process of tracking statistics and performance from the data gathered and then using this information to make specific decisions in order to improve the effectiveness of the channel. This section discusses different methods for tracking performance data and how to use this data to make informed decisions to improve video performance.

Experimenting and Iterating for Improvement

The insight is often gained after an analysis of various A/B tests that the best course of action is not always to make a single change to a video, but to try a few changes to identify a combination that yields the best results. An example of this is a study conducted with producers from the Sesame Workshop looking to increase the viewership of classic video clips from Sesame Street. By trying various hosting designs and video annotations, an iteration of changes was found which doubled viewership of the content.

Experimenting and iterating for improvement are vital activities for increasing the effectiveness and performance of a video. The ways that different segments of viewers respond to video changes can often be revealed by looking at the relative metrics across those viewer segments. In the previous mention of a homepage redesign, an economic way to measure the success of the redesign would have been to test if a higher proportion of people click through to content by measuring the change in CTR only for those viewers that would have been part of the experimental condition.

Staying Up-to-Date with Algorithm Changes

There are various ways to learn about algorithm changes such as YouTube's Creator Academy and any news updates within the industry. YouTube's Creator Academy is a great tool to understand general optimization for video success and although it doesn't particularly outline the changes specifically made to the algorithm, keeping the information in mind definitely helps to discern uses of algorithm changes that can be found out through testing. Taking note of updates from the official YouTube blog or reliable news sources within the industry such as will outline specific changes made to the algorithm and how they may affect video discovery and what actions can be taken in response. Focusing on changes in trends in video metrics or the site layout could also give an idea of changes made to the algorithm and what changes in video optimization should be made as a result.

Another important aspect of understanding the algorithm is staying up to date with the constant changes. The YouTube algorithm changes quite frequently (with a minimum of 5 major updates each year), and every change made, big or small, affects how videos are discovered and their success potential. To continue understanding the algorithm, it's important to take note of changes made to video success.

YouTube Creator Academy

It's important to note that some courses may become quickly outdated if the algorithm sees significant changes, so it's good to stick to the more universal topics. YouTube will likely do its best to update the courses, but this is not guaranteed.

Courses are a combination of a mix of resources: videos, articles, infographics, and checklists. Courses are also built around a framework of 'learn best practices', 'put it into practice', 'measure & adapt'. This will help make the information more actionable and even provide scope for course takers to discuss what they're learning. A course can range from 1 hour to 3 hours depending on the depth of the topic.

The YouTube Creator Academy is YouTube's official resource for comprehensive courses on how to create great content, grow your channel, and optimize your channel. Courses are divided into 3 levels: Bronze (starting out), Silver (time to get serious), and Gold (taking it to the next level). They are further divided into 6 'academies' (categories), and there are plenty of courses per academy.

Industry News and Updates

Subscribing to a number of these sources by RSS, following them with an RSS application, or adding their associated Twitter accounts to TweetDeck will allow for quick and simple browsing of any recent algorithm changes. If changes have been made that are known to have affected video views, it is important to experiment to try to understand the changes. The most efficient way to do this is to make changes to the SEO of underperforming videos and see what impact the changes have had. This can be a good indicator of whether the changes that have been made are positive or negative for the ranking of certain videos.

YouTube and its parent company, Google, release press releases and have blogs that provide information on changes in the algorithms. The YouTube Creator Blog is a good starting point and sometimes provides links to more detailed information. The Google blog, or some of the inside search blogs, will also give insight into changes in the search and discovery algorithms. Marketing blogs and websites are another good source of information, as changes to the search and discovery algorithms often greatly impact video views. Being a recent addition to the internet marketing mix, information on changes to the search and discovery (SEO) aspects of videos is not always easy to come by. As the video and video marketing industries continue to grow, it is likely there will be more sources of information on algorithm changes in the future.

Learning from Successful YouTube Channels

A great starting point for researching successful channels in your niche is YouTube's "On The Rise" feature, which is updated on a monthly basis. This features 4 different content creators in the US and Canada, with separate features for Brazil and Germany. Chosen creators will see a sizable increase in viewership and subscribers in a short timeframe and often have less than 10,000 subscribers. YouTube also spotlights "Creators on the Rise" in the trending tab. Dubbed "a new weekly feature that recognizes and promotes rising talent on YouTube," this is a great way to find popular channels while the feature above is better for finding less-known creators.

It's important to note that "success" is somewhat relative, especially on a platform as diverse as YouTube. A channel focused on acquiring new leads for a consulting business might consider a video successful if it brings in 5 new clients, whereas a gamer might consider a video successful if it hits 20,000 views. In this case, we're referring to success as producing videos that attract a large audience and keep them coming back for more.

There's a wealth of valuable knowledge to be gained from monitoring and analyzing successful YouTube channels. As the old saying goes, "Success leaves clues." By identifying common strategies and tactics employed by top-performing channels in your niche, you can gain a better understanding of what it takes to produce popular content. With a little reverse engineering, you can apply those same tactics and put your own spin on it to increase the likelihood of your videos being discovered and viewed.

CHAPTER 10

Conclusion

This essay sets out to explore the impact of the YouTube algorithm, from psychological to social effects. It has been established that the YouTube algorithm is powerful and has the potential to cause social consequences. This is evident in the changes in video content, the rise of social media platforms, and the political arena. The algorithm has also been known to cause filter bubbles and algorithmic personalization, which are potential negative social implications caused by the algorithm. With the increasing use of YouTube as the new TV and the use of it for learning (especially in the younger generation), it is essential to take a further look into the algorithm and its future effects. Although YouTube may not be the cause for the social changes, it certainly plays a big role in shaping the information society today.